GETTING TO KNOW THE WORLD'S GREATEST ARTISTS

P I E T E R
BRUEGEL

WRITTEN AND ILLUSTRATED BY MIKE VENEZIA

CONSULTANT MEG MOSS

CHILDRENS PRESS®
CHICAGO

For Liz and Mike

Cover: *Peasant Wedding Feast.* c. 1567-68. Oil on wood panel, 44⅞ x 64⅛ inches. Kunsthistorisches Museum, Vienna, Austria.

Library of Congress Cataloging-in-Publication Data

Venezia, Mike.
    Pieter Bruegel / written & illustrated by Mike Venezia.
        p.   cm. — (Getting to know the world's greatest artists)
    Summary: Briefly examines the life and work of the sixteenth-century Flemish painter, describing and giving examples of his art.
    ISBN 0-516-02279-2
    1. Bruegel, Pieter, ca. 1525-1569 — Juvenile literature.
[1. Bruegel, Pieter, ca. 1525-1569. 2. Artists.
3. Painting, Flemish. 4. Art appreciation.] I. Title.
II. Series: Venezia, Mike. Getting to know the world's greatest artists.
ND673.B73V48 1992
760'.092 — dc20   92-4810
[B]   CIP
                                                              AC

Detail of *Peasant Wedding Feast* on page 25.

Pieter Bruegel was born sometime around 1527 near Antwerp, a city in the country now called Belgium. Except for what people can tell from his drawings and paintings, very little is known about Pieter Bruegel's life.

3

Pieter Bruegel probably learned about art in the workshop of Pieter Coecke van Aelst, a famous artist in Antwerp.

No one knew it at the time, but when Pieter Coecke van Aelst's little daughter, Mayken, grew up, she and Bruegel would fall in love and get married.

Antwerp was a very important city
during Pieter Bruegel's time. People
from all over the world went there to
trade and to buy such things as
spices, books, and maps. They also

borrowed money from the city's
many banks. Wealthy people who
lived in Antwerp were always
looking for works of art to fill up the
large rooms of their mansions.

The Martyrdom of Saint Catherine. c. 1540. Anonymous. Oil on wood transferred to plywood, 24½ x 46⁹⁄₁₆ inches. Samuel H. Kress Collection, National Gallery of Art, Washington, D.C.

They were mainly interested in paintings of scenery, known as landscapes, and in the work of the great Italian artists of the time. In 1552, Pieter Bruegel decided to travel to Italy to see for himself how the Italian artists painted.

The Alba Madonna. c. 1510. By Raphael. Oil on wood transferred to canvas, 37¼ inches in diameter. Andrew W. Mellon Collection, National Gallery of Art, Washington, D.C.

Mountain Landscape. c. 1554-55. Pen and brown ink, brown wash, 14¹⁄₁₆ x 17½ inches.
The Pierpont Morgan Library, New York. 1952.25.

In Italy, Bruegel probably learned
how artists such as Michelangelo and
Raphael painted people in a more
natural, three-dimensional way. But
the drawings from Bruegel's trip
show he was mainly interested in the
scenery he saw along the way,
especially the beautiful mountains.

Gluttony. 1558. An engraving by Pierre Van der Heyden based on Pieter Bruegel's
original drawing of 1557, 87⅝ x 115 ³/₁₀ inches.
© Bibliothèque Royale Albert I ᵉʳ , (Cabinet des Estampes), Brussels, Belgium.

When Pieter Bruegel returned from his trip, he didn't start to paint right away. He decided instead to work for a well-known printer in Antwerp. The printer made copies of Pieter Bruegel's drawings and sold them to people all over Europe.

Garden of Earthly Delights. c. 1503-04. By Hieronymus Bosch. Central panel of triptych, detail of upper central part, oil on wood panel, 86⅝ x 76¾ inches. Prado, Madrid, Spain. Giraudon/Art Resource, New York.

Some of Bruegel's prints show that he was influenced by the work of an earlier great artist, Hieronymus Bosch. Pieter Bruegel loved Bosch's strange scenes filled with weird creatures. Sometimes it's hard to tell the two artists' works apart.

The Parable of the Sower. 1557. Oil on panel, 29 x 40½ inches.
Putnam Foundation, Timken Museum of Art, San Diego, California.

Most of Bruegel's first paintings were landscapes. He combined the scenery near his home with the mountains and valleys he remembered from his trip to Italy.

Landscape with the Fall of Icarus. c. 1567-68.
Oil on wood transferred to canvas, 29 x 44⅛ inches.
Musées Royaux des Beaux-Arts, Brussels, Belgium.
Scala/Art Resource, New York.

Bruegel was very interested in
landscapes, but he also enjoyed
painting people. He added more
people to his works as time went on.

Many of Bruegel's works of art show his great interest in the poor people who lived out in the countryside.

These people were known as peasants. Sometimes Bruegel painted them hard at work—planting, growing, or harvesting crops.

The Harvesters. 1565.
Oil on wood, 63¼ x 46½ inches.
Rogers Fund, 1919, The
Metropolitan Museum of Art,
New York.

Detail of *The Wedding Dance*. c. 1566. Oil on panel, 47 x 62 inches.
City of Detroit Purchase, © The Detroit Institute of Arts,
1991, Detroit, Michigan.

Other times he would show them
having fun during a holiday or a
special occasion.

Even though Bruegel came from a
large city, he knew a lot about how

the poor country people lived. One
story tells how he and a friend would
dress up like peasants and sneak into
their parties. Sometimes they even
brought gifts along.

In this painting, Bruegel showed people acting out proverbs. A proverb is a short saying that teaches a lesson. In the 1500s, many people expected a good painting to teach them a lesson and be filled with lots of interesting things to look at. Bruegel's painting did both things very well.

Netherlandish Proverbs. 1559. Oil on panel, 46 x 64⅛ inches. Gemäldegalerie, Staatliche Museen Preußischer Kulturbesitz, Berlin, Germany.

Many of the proverbs of Bruegel's time are still familiar today. For instance, the man in the lower left is butting his head against a brick wall, and the lady in the lower right is crying over spilt milk.

Many experts think that Bruegel may have put important secret messages in some of his paintings; messages that only he and a few others knew about. Sometimes these paintings included strange and frightening symbols and images.

Dulle Griet. c. 1562-64.
Oil on wood, 17 x 11⅞ inches.
Museum Mayer Van Den Bergh,
Antwerp, Belgium.

Massacre of the Innocents. c. 1566. Oil on wood panel, 45⅝ x 63 inches.
Kunsthistorisches Museum, Vienna, Austria.

Bruegel disguised the messages in some of his paintings because he lived during a very dangerous time. If you offended the wrong person, you could get into real trouble. The painting of the Bible story above may have been a way of showing the cruelty of the Spanish king, who was ruling Bruegel's country at that time.

Children's Games. 1560. Oil on wood panel, 46½ x 63⅜ inches.
Kunsthistorisches Museum, Vienna, Austria.

Children's Games may also contain a
secret message. Bruegel may have
been showing that the people who
ran his city and ruled its churches
were acting like children and not
taking their jobs seriously.

Peasant Dance. c. 1566-67. Oil on wood panel, 44⅞ x 64½ inches.
Kunsthistorisches Museum, Vienna, Austria.

Two of Bruegel's most famous
paintings show that he was able to
paint people as naturally and three-
dimensionally as the great Italian
artists. Bruegel's paintings were
different, though, because he painted
real, everyday people instead of the

Peasant Wedding Feast. c. 1567-68. Oil on wood panel, 44⅞ x 64⅛ inches.
Kunsthistorisches Museum, Vienna, Austria.

mythological gods, angels, and
famous heroes that the Italian artists
were known for. Pieter Bruegel was
also able to capture special moments
in time, just as a good photographer
is able to do.

Hunters in the Snow is one of a group of paintings Bruegel did to show the different seasons of the year. It's interesting to look at the beautiful scenery and the activities going on all over the countryside. But it's the way Bruegel makes you almost *feel* the chilly winter weather that makes this one of his greatest paintings.

Hunters in the Snow. 1565.
Oil on wood panel, 46 x 63¾ inches.
Kunsthistorisches Museum, Vienna, Austria.

Pieter Bruegel's family was filled with artists. His wife's mother and father were both well-known painters of the day.

Landscape Under Snow.
by Pieter Bruegel
the Younger,
$16\frac{1}{8}$ x $22\,^{7}/_{10}$ inches.
Galleria Doria Pamphili,
Rome, Italy.
Scala/Art Resource,
New York.

*A Woodland Road with
Travelers* by Jan Bruegel.
1607. Oil on wood,
$32\frac{3}{4}$ x $18\frac{1}{8}$ inches.
Purchase, Fletcher,
Rogers, Pfeiffer, Dodge,
Harris Brisbane Dick,
and Louis V. Bell Funds,
Joseph Pulitzer Bequest,
1974, The Metropolitan
Museum of Art, New York.

Bruegel's two sons also became
famous artists, but neither of them
quite had their father's imagination
or were able to put the same kind of
human feeling into their paintings.

Because Pieter Bruegel created his own special style of art and often didn't go along with the fashion of the day, his paintings weren't always popular.

Detail of *Adoration of the Magi in the Snow*. 1567. Oil on panel, 13¾ x 21⅝ inches. Oskar Reinhart Collection, Winterthur, Switzerland.

Pieter Bruegel died in 1569. For many years after, people thought that he was just a fun-loving artist who wanted to make people

Detail of *Battle Between Carnival and Lent*. 1559. Oil on wood panel, 46½ x 64¾ inches. Kunsthistorisches Museum, Vienna, Austria.

laugh. But Pieter Bruegel did much more than that. He was able to paint scary as well as beautiful things, and show what the people he painted might have been like in real life.

Detail of *Peasant Wedding Feast* on page 25.

Maybe more than any other great artist, Pieter Bruegel created unforgettable art that is just plain fun to look at.

The Tower of Babel. 1563.
Oil on wood panel, 44⅞ x 61 inches.
Kunsthistorisches Museum, Vienna, Austria.

When people look at a Pieter Bruegel painting, they often think he used very few colors. At first glance, his pictures seem to be an overall brown or gray or dark yellow. But if you look closely, you'll be surprised to find that Bruegel used lots of bright reds, blues, greens, and even pinks.

Detail of
Children's Games
on page 23.

The paintings in this book came from the museums listed below.

Bibliothèque Royale Albert Ier,
  Brussels, Belgium
The Detroit Institute of Arts,
  Detroit, Michigan
Galleria Doria Pamphili,
  Rome, Italy
Kunsthistorisches Museum,
  Vienna, Austria
The Metropolitan Museum of Art,
  New York, New York
Museum Mayer Van Den Bergh,
  Antwerp, Belgium

National Gallery of Art,
  Washington, D.C.
Oskar Reinhart Collection,
  Winterthur, Switzerland
The Pierpont Morgan Library,
  New York, New York
Prado, Madrid, Spain
Royal Museums of Fine Arts,
  Brussels, Belgium
Staatliche Museen Preußischer
  Kulturbesitz, Berlin, Germany
Timken Museum of Art,
  San Diego, California